The Power of the
Merchant Navies

An unidentified unrebuilt 'Merchant Navy' in blue livery takes water at the west end of Platform 4 at Salisbury at the head of the down 'Atlantic Coast Express' in the early 1950s. Engine-changing on Waterloo-West of England expresses ceased at Salisbury in 1950, but crew changes continued. *G. Heiron*

The Power of the
Merchant Navies

Gavin Morrison

An imprint of
Ian Allan Publishing

Contents

Frontispiece:
Rebuilt No 35013 *Blue Funnel Certum Pete Finem* blows off at Bournemouth shed on 26 March 1967. *Gavin Morrison*

Title page:
No 35010 *Blue Star* on Eastleigh shed on 8 September 1964. *Gavin Morrison*

First published 2007

ISBN (10) 0 86093 607 4
ISBN (13) 978 0 86093 607 7

© Ian Allan Publishing Ltd 2007

Published by Oxford Publishing Co

an imprint of Ian Allan Publishing Ltd, Hersham, Surrey KT12 4RG.
Printed in England by Ian Allan Printing Ltd, Hersham, Surrey KT12 4RG.

Code: 0706/A3

Visit the Ian Allan Publishing website at www.ianallanpublishing.com

Introduction

Under the able leadership of Sir Herbert Walker, during the mid-1930s the Southern Railway had concentrated on electrifying the lines to the immediate south of London to improve its commuter services, which were and still are the backbone of the railway; as a result the era of glamorous high-speed trains hauled by streamlined engines had passed the railway by.

With the realisation that the Second World War was inevitable, the SR saw that it was heading for trouble unless it did something about its steam locomotive stock to cope with wartime requirements; by comparison with other railways, it consisted of relatively small and underpowered designs. That is not to say that the famous 'King Arthur' class were not excellent locomotives relative to their size, and the 'Schools' were brilliant 4-4-0s, but something much larger and more powerful was needed, and quickly.

Maunsell, who had served the railway well, tended his resignation on 27 May 1937, and it was arranged in advance that Oliver Vaughan Snell Bulleid would be the new Chief Mechanical Engineer; on 4 June 1937 the announcement of his appointment was duly made in the railway press. Initially he made some modifications to the 'King Arthurs' (Urie batch), 'Lord Nelsons' and 'Schools' by fitting the Lemaitre blastpipe system, which helped their performance.

Bulleid then turned his efforts to the design of a large new locomotive, and matters moved quickly. A 4-8-2 was considered but rejected due to weight, and a 2-8-2 design was nearly built, but eventually a Pacific design was selected. Having been Sir Nigel Gresley's number two at Doncaster, Bulleid persuaded C. S. Cocks, a draughtsman there, to come and join him at Eastleigh. The board gave the go-ahead for ten new Pacifics in March 1938, although it appears that the exact design was not specified, and he was warned by the Chief Civil Engineer to keep the weight as light as possible – a figure of 92½ tons was considered as acceptable.

British locomotive design had changed very little since the Great Western had built its 'Star' and '28xx' classes around 1903; although designs had evolved to produce larger and more powerful locomotives, nothing revolutionary had taken place until the appearance of 'Merchant Navy' *Channel Packet* in 1941. Having read many excellent books on the class, which are listed in the Bibliography, it does not seem clear to me whether the Southern Railway board was encouraging Bulleid to design, or even realising that he was designing, such a revolutionary locomotive. Considering that the locomotives were desperately needed for war conditions and workloads, one would have thought that something relatively conventional and likely to work without problem would have been appropriate, but these were obviously not Bulleid's thoughts.

The locomotives were proposed on the basis of being 'mixed traffic', as it was not thought appropriate to be seen to be building a new express passenger engine design in wartime. The end result must have come as a big surprise to officials on the Southern, and to the fitters and maintenance staff at Salisbury, where it was decided to base the locomotives. They must have appeared like something out of *Star Wars*!

Needless to say with such a revolutionary design, it took staff a very long time to become accustomed to the class. Everything had been designed to reduce maintenance and achieve greater availability, but initially the end results were exactly the opposite; in fact, the locomotives were failing so often in traffic that they were kept on freight duties, which at least justified their 'mixed traffic' status. Moreover, there was one major problem: instead of the estimated 92tons 10cwt, *Channel Packet* weighed in at 99tons 10cwt, which was unacceptable.

Many books have been written on the advantages and problems of the locomotives – a boiler operating at 280psi, the 'thermic syphons', steel fireboxes and, of course, the chain-driven valve gear in an oil bath, not to mention the air-smoothed casing. Even the numbering was different, 21C1 must have caused confusion, the 'C' indicating the number of driving axles (third letter of the alphabet), '2' and '1' the front and rear bogie axles, and the last number(s) being the individual locomotive number, but as this is a photographic album I do not propose to expand on these in any great detail.

As time passed, and crews became familiar with the 'Merchant Navies', they realised what fantastic locomotives they were, when they were working. They steamed probably better than any other locomotive in the country, rode very well and had comfortable cabs, even if they were rather hot in summer. However, the cost was high and they consumed a lot of water and coal, not to mention the cost of oil, estimated at 2 gallons per 100 miles. The problem of excessive weight was never really solved, although it was reduced, then, no doubt due to the need for the locomotives during the war, was overlooked. There were major problems involving smoke obscuring the crew's vision, which was never really solved despite many experiments, and oil leaking from the oil bath, which encouraged violent slipping with disastrous results, very occasionally catching fire. In summary, I think it is fair to say that the footplate crews liked them for their power, free steaming and ride, whereas the maintenance staff considered them very hard and unpleasant to maintain (oil everywhere!).

Bulleid departed from the SR after nationalisation in 1949, and the management of the Southern Region of British Railways was not slow in examining the costs involved in keeping the class running. The potentially

Below:
Unrebuilt No 35019 *French Line CGT* rests in between duties on the ashpits at Nine Elms shed on 13 September 1958. *Gavin Morrison*

disastrous crank axle failure of No 35020 at Crewkerne in 1953 – with others also found to be dangerous – probably resulted in the decision to rebuild the class, although withdrawal had been seriously considered.

R. G. Jarvis was asked to prepare a rebuild design, which was done; it retained the boiler (but with pressure reduced to 250psi), frames, outside cylinders, wheels and cab, but the valve gear, piston heads, oil bath and 'air-smoothed' casing were all to go. No 35018 *British India Line* was selected to be the first candidate, as it was said never to have been the best of locomotives, and it duly emerged from Eastleigh Works, looking very different, in February 1956. Costings were done, with recovery of the cost estimated to be achieved by 1962, and they were expected to have lasted longer than 1967, when Southern steam finished. On the whole they proved to be reliable, although still tended to consume a fair amount of coal if driven hard, and apparently did not ride quite as well as the unrebuilt examples; however, with availability improved and the cost of maintenance reduced, they put in good service before the end finally came. The rebuilds covered only low mileages, the last, No 35030, achieving only 499,642 miles in its rebuilt state, while No 35029 travelled only 748,343 miles in total.

There was hope that No 35022 (one of the 11 preserved examples) would be rebuilt to its original form, but currently this is not going to happen. Fortunately there are several unrebuilt 'West Countries' and 'Battle of Britains' around, so today's enthusiasts can still enjoy and wonder at these controversial locomotives.

Those who worked on the unrebuilt locomotives must be getting fewer in number, and no doubt as the years progress the stories surrounding them will become embellished. Fortunately, as already mentioned there are excellent books devoted to the class, and from which most of the information I have included has been obtained, so my grateful thanks go to the authors.

I can claim to have seen every Bulleid Pacific in its unrebuilt form, but this was from intensive 'shed-bashing', and I can clearly remember seeing No 35024 in lined blue

Above:
A selection of the cast metal nameplates carried by the 'Merchant Navy' class.

livery at Exeter – how I wish I had seen one in that livery at the head of the 'Golden Arrow' ready to leave Victoria.

It would be crazy to devote a book to the tenders, as there were constant alterations to them over the years, so I have included brief details in the captions concerning the variations.

Once again my thanks go to all the photographers who clearly spent a lot of time covering the unrebuilt 'Merchant Navies', as well as the rebuilds, as there is certainly no shortage of excellent pictures.

This album is primarily a photographic record of these remarkable locomotives and is unlikely to provide any new information about them, but what is certain is that the history of British steam locomotives would have been far less interesting without the contribution made by Oliver Bulleid.

Gavin Morrison
Mirfield

Bibliography

Bradley, D. C. *Locomotives of the Southern Railway*, Part 2 (RCTS, 1976)

Denny, R. *The Book of Merchant Navy Pacifics* (Irwell Press, 2001)

Fry. A. J. *Bulleid Power* (Alan Sutton, 1990)

Locomotives Illustrated Part 12 (Ian Allan)

Morrison, B. and Creer, S. *Power of the Bulleid Pacifics* (OPC, 1983)

Right:
An official portrait of No 21C1 *Channel Packet*, taken after it was repainted back into Malachite Green in December 1945. It still retains the cast metal Southern plates on the tender and '21C1' on the cabside, but the former horseshoe-shaped Southern plate on the smokebox has been replaced by a fully circular one. The locomotive is now fitted with short smoke deflector plates, although the original cylinder casing is still retained. The front number plate is in the vertical position, rather than sloped as originally.

Channel Packet was allocated to the Eastern section in April 1946 and was used to haul a special publicity working of the 'Golden Arrow' on the 13th of that month. It then headed the first public working on the 15th. *Rail Archive Stephenson*

Centre right:
No 35019 *French Line CGT* is seen on Eastleigh shed on 24 February 1962, awaiting a visit to the works. *Gavin Morrison*

Below:
A fine portrait of No 21C14 *Nederland Line* in Malachite Green livery at an unknown location, with short smoke deflectors. The date is not recorded, but is probably November 1945, when the original black livery was replaced by the green. *Rail Archive Stephenson/O. J. Morris*

Below:

An official picture of No 21C1 *Channel Packet* at Eastleigh Works in March 1941. Note the sloping front number plate, and the cast number plate and 'Southern' plate on the tender. It is fitted with the horseshoe-shaped 'Southern' plate on the smokebox. The aperture through which the sandboxes were filled is shown to the front of the centre driving wheel, and the chimney cover can also just be seen. The locomotive spent its initial months at Eastleigh being extensively tested, and was named at the works by the then Minister of Transport, the Rt Hon J. T. C. MooreBrabazon, on 10 March 1941. It was attached to a 5,000-gallon tender. *Ian Allan Library*

21C1 *Channel Packet*	
Renumbered:	35001
New:	February 1941
Mileage, unrebuilt:	807,318
Allocations:	Salisbury, June 1941; Exmouth Junction, autumn 1942; Stewarts Lane, April 1946; Exmouth Junction, April 1946; Stewarts Lane, 25 January 1957; Nine Elms, 14 June 1959; Bournemouth, 14 September 1964
Liveries:	Matt Malachite Green when new; Malachite Green; BR Blue, October 1949; BR Green, May 1952
Withdrawn:	22 November 1964
Total mileage:	1,095,884
Fate:	Scrapped at Bird's, Morriston, Swansea, by April 1965

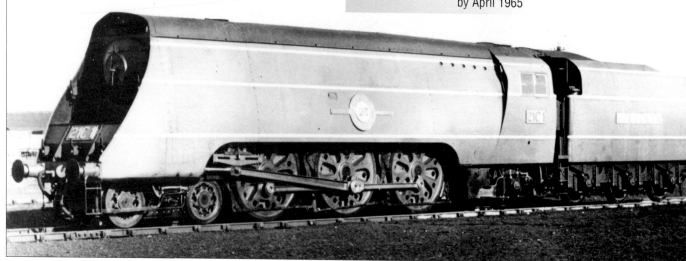

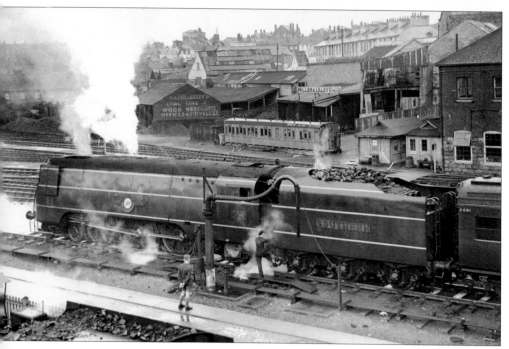

Left:

This superbly atmospheric photograph shows the surrounds of Exeter Central station in 1947. A lone young enthusiast looks on as No 21C1 *Channel Packet* prepares to leave with an up Waterloo express. It still retains the cabside and tender plates, and is now fitted with short smoke deflectors. In April 1946 *Channel Packet* was allocated to Stewarts Lane shed for a couple of weeks and, after some test runs, hauled a publicity special prior to the reintroduction of the 'Golden Arrow' on 15 April. It then returned to Exmouth Junction. *Rail Archive Stephenson, R. S. Clarke*

Right:
After working the up 'Atlantic Coast Express', *Channel Packet* awaits servicing on the ashpits at Nine Elms shed on 24 April 1954. By now it carries its BR number and has lost the fairing in front of the cylinders; it also has the larger smoke deflectors and modified cab, and the two apertures for sand can be clearly seen above the nameplate. No 35001 has had at least three boiler changes since the previous picture. *Gavin Morrison*

Below:
In fine external condition the rebuilt *Channel Packet* approaches Exeter Central with the car-carrying train from Surbiton to the West Country on 20 August 1960. *Rail Archive Stephenson, M. J. Fox*

Above:
Not a normal working for a 'Merchant Navy', *Channel Packet* passes Weybridge on 12 October 1964 with some empty electric multiple unit stock for Eastleigh. It is running with a rebodied 5,250-gallon tender.
D. A. Buckett

Left:
No 35001 has been prepared on Weymouth shed for an evening up Waterloo express on 20 April 1962. I don't think they could have fitted any more coal into the tender!
Gavin Morrison

Left:
Later that same day, the level of coal in the tender has been slightly reduced as *Channel Packet*, leaking badly, passes Radipole Halt just outside Weymouth with the evening up express. The steep 3-mile gradient of 1 in 74/50 to Bincombe Tunnel will present no problem for the locomotive with only six coaches. *Gavin Morrison*

Right:
No 21C2 *Union Castle* is seen in June 1949 climbing Honiton Bank with a down West of England express. The original horseshoe-shaped 'Southern' smokebox plate was replaced by the circular type seen here in February 1942. The cast plate front number was positioned vertically on No 21C2, rather than the sloping position on No 21C1. The locomotive is now fitted with smoke deflector plates, but it managed to retain its cabside and tender plates until renumbered in January 1950. The lined Malachite Green livery was in a poor state by this date. *P. Ransome-Wallis*

21C2 *Union Castle*

Renumbered:	35002, January 1950
New:	June 1946
Mileage, unrebuilt:	776,797
Allocations:	Salisbury when new; Exmouth Junction, autumn 1942; Bournemouth, 13 May 1954; Exmouth Junction, 22 June 1954; Bournemouth, 6 June 1958; Nine Elms, 24 November 1960; Bournemouth, 17 January 1961; Nine Elms, 27 January 1964
Liveries:	Unlined Matt Malachite Green; lined Matt Malachite before 4 July 1941; Black, May 1944; Malachite Green, July 1946; BR Blue, January 1950; BR Green, June 1951
Withdrawn:	February 1964
Total mileage:	1,101,194
Fate:	Scrapped at Slag Reductions Co, Rotherham, December 1964

Below:
Unfortunately there are no details for this picture, but it clearly shows *Union Castle* ready to leave Waterloo with a down express. An 'M7' 0-4-4T simmers alongside ready to remove some empty stock. Soon after *Union Castle* was repainted in BR Green it was paired with a blue tender.

Like No 21C1, No 21C2 was used extensively on both passenger and freight trials in 1941, and on 17 October 1947 it was tested with a 16-coach train between Waterloo and Bournemouth running non-stop in both directions. *Ian Allan Library*

21C4 *Cunard White Star*

Renumbered:	35004, April 1948
New:	October 1941
Mileage, unrebuilt:	750,886
Allocations:	Salisbury when new; Exmouth Junction, 1942; Salisbury, 13 November 1948; Exmouth Junction, 4 February 1950; Salisbury, 1 April 1957; Bournemouth, 14 September 1964
Liveries:	Malachite Green when new; Black, July 1943; Malachite Green, April 1946; BR Blue, October 1950; BR Green, February 1953
Withdrawn:	October 1965
Total mileage:	1,131,417
Fate:	Scrapped by Cohen's at Eastleigh Works, February 1966

Left:
This fine picture of *Cunard White Star* heading the up 'Devon Belle' near Templecombe in 1947 clearly shows the curved casing in front of the cylinders. Also visible is the strengthening rib along the casing. It is odd that the Southern Railway originally painted the locomotives in Malachite Green when new during the war, then painted them Black after a short period. On 30 November 1942 the locomotive had come under fire from German aircraft near Whimple while working the 10.10am Plymouth-Brighton train. *Ian Allan Library*

Below left:
Now back in Malachite Green from Black, No 21C4 pulls away from Templecombe with an up West of England express in January 1948. *R. F. Roberts*

Below:
Now rebuilt, *Cunard White Star* stands at its home shed of Salisbury awaiting its next duty on 1 October 1961. *Gavin Morrison*

Above:
Still with the 'Southern' circular plaque on the smokebox, and therefore the new BR number above the buffer beam, *Cunard White Star* is being serviced on Exmouth Junction shed's ashpits. It still has the original cab and full canopy over the cylinders, but is in Malachite Green livery with 'British Railways' on the tender, which means that the photograph must have been taken between January 1948 and October 1950. *Pendragon collection*

Left:
Cunard White Star departs from Salisbury with the down 7.33am Waterloo-West of England express on 9 August 1958 as No 35014 *Nederland Line* arrives with the 7.30am from Exeter to Waterloo. No 35004 had emerged from Eastleigh Works only the previous month after rebuilding. *S. Creer*

Below:
While still allocated to Salisbury, *Cunard White Star* passes clear signals on the gantry near Fleet while heading a down West of England express on 14 May 1964. No 35004 was withdrawn prematurely after a severe slip near Hook on 28 October 1965, which resulted in broken and bent coupling rods, in spite of the fact that it had only recently visited Eastleigh Works. It was one of the few members of the class not allocated to Nine Elms shed. *Rail Archive Stephenson, D. M. C. Hepburne-Scott*

21C5 *Canadian Pacific*

Renumbered:	S35005, March 1968 (the only member of the class to carry the 'S' prefix)
New:	December 1941
Mileage, unrebuilt:	632,322
Allocations:	Salisbury when new; Exmouth Junction, 1942; Nine Elms, 13 November 1948; Exmouth Junction, 12 May 1951; Nine Elms, 19 March 1954; Bournemouth, 26 November 1959; Weymouth
Liveries:	Malachite Green; Black, March 1942; Malachite Green, January 1946; BR Blue, February 1950; BR Green, February 1954
Withdrawn:	10 October 1965
Total mileage:	976,806
Fate:	Sold to Woodham Bros, Barry, for scrapping, but passed into preservation in March 1973, eventually returning to main-line working.

Above:
Still with the 'Southern' plaque on the smokebox, but renumbered 35005 with 'British Railways' on the tender, *Canadian Pacific* rushes through Winchfield at the head of the down 'Atlantic Coast Express' on 2 September 1949. In spite of wartime conditions, special naming ceremonies were held, mainly at Southampton Docks, although No 21C5, repainted Black for the occasion, was named at Victoria on 27 March 1942. The locomotive hauled the first regular 16-coach working from Exeter to Waterloo on 4 May 1943. *Rail Archive Stephenson, E. C. Griffith*

Left:
This picture is undated, but it was taken before *Canadian Pacific* received the BR Blue livery in February 1950. It is in the same condition as the previous picture, but this time is passing Brookwood station on the down 'ACE'. *R. F. Dearden*

Below left:
This interesting picture of *Canadian Pacific* shows it carrying out one of the 'mixed traffic' duties for which the class was originally built. In its fine BR Blue livery it must have been an unusual sight shunting milk tankers at Clapham Junction on 21 June 1951. *Brian Morrison*

Above right:
After receiving its blue livery, *Canadian Pacific* was sent to the Rugby testing station in February 1950, returning to Nine Elms the following month. It is seen during March on Rugby shed alongside a Midland 0-4-4T. It was then trialled with the mobile LMR testing unit, and during this period was fitted with a Berkley mechanical stoker, which it retained until April 1951; the tender top was raised to compensate for loss of capacity due to the mechanical stoker. Disaster struck in September 1950 when the chain drive parted, destroying the oil bath and motion. In 1954 the boiler pressure was reduced to 250psi. *Rail Archive Stephenson, W. J. V. Anderson*

Above:
Canadian Pacific is nearly blowing off as it climbs the 1 in 176 across Brockenhurst Common with the down 'Royal Wessex' on 4 June 1960. *Hugh Ballantyne*

Left:
On 13 July 1962, looking very clean after a recent visit to Eastleigh Works for a light intermediate repair, *Canadian Pacific* stands at the east end of Bournemouth Central with an up Waterloo express while its tender is filled. *H. C. Casserley*

No 35006 *Peninsular & Oriental SN Co* approaches Walton-on-Thames with the down 11.54 Waterloo-Salisbury local on 11 November 1950; the signals are ex-LSWR lattice-post brackets. The locomotive has a smokebox number plate and 'British Railways' on the tender, although it did run with the BR number and 'Southern' on the tender for a short period. *Peninsular & Oriental SN Co* was the only member of the class to remain at the same shed throughout its career; it also stayed attached to the same tender, No 3116. In December 1942, while working an up freight near Honiton, the chain parted in the oil bath, resulting in fires that needed attention from the local fire brigade. *E. D. Bruton*

21C6 *Peninsular & Oriental SN Co*

Renumbered:	35006, December 1948
New:	December 1941
Mileage, unrebuilt:	962,757
Allocations:	Salisbury from new
Liveries:	Malachite Green when new; Black, May 1942; Malachite Green, September 1946; BR Blue, March 1951; BR Green, September 1953
Withdrawn:	August 1964
Total mileage:	1,134,319
Fate:	Sent for scrapping to Woodham Bros, Barry, but left in March 1983 for preservation

Left:
The casing in front of the cylinders has been removed as No 35006, in terrible external condition, pulls out of Yeovil Junction with an express for Waterloo on 5 June 1959. Rebuilding was to take place the following October. An 'M7' 0-4-4T waits in the bay at the head of the connecting service to Yeovil Pen Mill. *J. A. Coiley*

Left:
Another fine picture of *Orient Line* in BR Blue livery shows it near Winchfield during May 1950 with a West of England express. Note that all three apertures for sand for the driving wheels are open. The locomotive is running with the standard three-window-type cab, which it received during a works visit in April 1949. *M. W. Earley*

Below left:
During the electrification of the Bournemouth line, the Bournemouth and Weymouth expresses were regularly diverted via the steeply graded Alton to Winchester Junction line, which included Medstead Bank, now part of the Mid-Hants Railway. The 10.30 Waterloo-Weymouth train, headed by No 35008 *Orient Line*, is seen tackling the gradient on the single line on 1 May 1966. *W. G. Sumner*

Above right:
Orient Line passes under the Bournemouth line at Battledown flyover, just west of Basingstoke, with an up express from Salisbury. *R. Russell*

Right:
In clean condition while allocated to Bournemouth, *Orient Line* heads the up Weymouth portion of a Waterloo express between Gas Works Junction and Bournemouth Central on 1 August 1962. *Gavin Morrison*

Right:
With still a year to go before the end of steam on the Southern Region, No 35008 makes a fine sight as it heads the up 13.25 Weymouth-Waterloo train near Shawford on 26 July 1966. *J. H. Bird*

Above:
Shaw Savill appears to have been one of the most camera-shy members of the class, but here we have a fine shot of it at Waterloo ready to depart with a Plymouth train on 24 March 1951. The horizontal rib on the casing side is clearly shown – this was carried only by Nos 35003 to 35009. It was another member of the class never to be allocated to Nine Elms, and was also unusual as it ran with the same tender, No 3119, throughout its career. It was the first of the class to work a regular 16-coach train from Waterloo to Exeter on 4 May 1943. *Brian Morrison*

21C9 *Shaw Savill*

Renumbered:	35009, August 1949
New:	June 1942
Mileage, unrebuilt:	684,482
Allocations:	Salisbury when new; Exmouth Junction, 1 April 1957
Liveries:	Black when new; Malachite Green, November 1946; BR Blue, August 1949; BR Green, June 1954
Withdrawn:	September 1964
Total mileage:	1,127,542
Fate:	Sold to Woodham Bros, Barry, for scrapping, but passed into preservation in 1982

Right:
Shaw Savill is again seen in BR Blue livery, ready to leave Basingstoke with a West of England express during August 1952. *J. Davenport*

Below:
In rebuilt form, No 35009 heads the 10.48am Torrington-Waterloo portion of the 'Atlantic Coast Express' near Farnborough on 31 August 1963. *A. W. Martin*

Bottom:
Three months after rebuilding, *Shaw Savill* is still in immaculate condition at its home shed of Salisbury, where it was allocated for its first 15 years. *Rail Archive Stephenson, J. F. Davies*

Below:

The locomotive was placed in store at Bournemouth shed at least six weeks before being sent to Eastleigh Works for rebuilding, and it is seen there out of use on 11 November 1956. It was the first of the initial batch (order 1068) to be rebuilt, and during the rebuilding it was discovered to be in need of new main frames ahead of the cylinders.
C. P. Boocock

21C10 *Blue Star*

Renumbered:	35010, December 1948
New:	July 1942
Mileage, unrebuilt:	663,174
Allocations:	Salisbury when new; Nine Elms, 4 February 1950; Bournemouth, 29 January 1956; Exmouth Junction, 20 March 1960; Bournemouth, 14 September 1964
Liveries:	Black when new; Malachite Green, June 1947; BR Blue, November 1949; BR Green, November 1952
Withdrawn:	September 1966
Total mileage:	1,241,299
Fate:	Sent to Woodham Bros, Barry, for scrapping, but entered preservation in January 1985

Right:
Easy work for *Blue Star* as, in rebuilt
form, it departs from Wilton (South)
with the 3.35pm local from Yeovil
Junction to Salisbury on 30 July 1961.
Hugh Ballantyne

Left:
The shunter is ready to couple up the
van outside Axminster goods shed as
Blue Star eases the wagons forward
in the yard. As already mentioned,
Mr Bulleid intended the class to be
'mixed traffic', but one hardly believes
that he had this sort of work in mind!
W. P. Conolly

Below:
A view of *Blue Star* out of steam on
Eastleigh shed on 8 September 1964.
Gavin Morrison

Above:
No 21C11 is seen on Eastleigh shed during 1945, when less than a year old; it is painted Black and the casing in front of the cylinders is in place. Note again the openings on the side of the casing to feed the sanders. Short smoke deflectors are fitted, and the locomotive is attached to a 5,100-gallon tender. *Rail Archive Stephenson, A. W. Croughton*

21C11 *General Steam Navigation*

Renumbered:	35011, November 1948
New:	December 1944
Mileage, unrebuilt:	670,782
Allocations:	Nine Elms when new; Bournemouth, 8 February 1954; Nine Elms, 13 May 1954; Exmouth Junction, 12 June 1957; Bournemouth, 10 March 1960
Liveries:	Black when new; Malachite Green, January 1947; Brunswick Green, November 1951
Withdrawn:	February 1966
Total mileage:	1,069,128 miles
Fate:	Preserved

Left:
No 35011 *General Steam Navigation* heads the up 'Bournemouth Belle', with its large headboard, on the approach to Micheldever near the top of the long 21-mile climb, mainly at 1 in 252, from St Denys to Litchfield Tunnel. The locomotive was the first of the second batch of 'Merchant Navies' built to order No 1189 and attached to 5,100-gallon tenders; it is seen here in Malachite Green livery prior to 1951. *F. R. Hebron*

Above left:
Blue Funnel hurries an up West of England express along the main line between Basingstoke and Woking some time between November 1946, when it received the Malachite Green livery, and July 1948, when it was numbered 35013. *Rail Archive Stephenson, C. J. Grose*

Left:
In this very fine picture, No 35013 *Blue Funnel* is passing Winchfield at the head of the 14-coach all-Pullman 'Devon Belle', complete with headboard and side 'wings', on 2 September 1949. *Blue Funnel* will work the train non-stop to Wilton, where another 'Merchant Navy' will take over to Exeter. *Rail Archive Stephenson, E. C. Griffith*

Above:
Blue Funnel is receiving attention inside Eastleigh Works on 25 July 1956, two months after it was rebuilt. One of the Southern Region's Fairburn 2-6-4Ts can be seen behind it. *Brian Morrison*

Right:
The evening sun produces this dramatic picture of *Blue Funnel* at the head of the 6pm Waterloo-Exeter express at Salisbury on 12 May 1958. There was a 6-minute stop here to change crews and fill the tender with water. *Brian Morrison*

Left:
This interesting picture shows *Blue Funnel* coasting down the 1 in 252 through Micheldever station with the 13.30 Waterloo-Weymouth train on 18 March 1967. Note all the station facilities on a platform that is now devoid of tracks. *J. H. Bird*

Left:
Blue Funnel is shown ready to leave Bournemouth West with an up afternoon express for Waterloo on 31 August 1965. The coaches look immaculate, having no doubt been through the washing plant at the carriage sheds, but No 35013 hasn't seen an oily rag for some time! The 70F shed plate indicates that it is allocated to Bournemouth, the more familiar code of 71B having been altered in September 1963. *Gavin Morrison*

Below left:
The New Forest ponies are perfectly positioned in this picture of a very dirty No 35013 heading the 'Bournemouth Belle' past Lyndhurst Road in the heart of the Forest on 8 August 1966. Although *Blue Funnel* was the name chosen, the locomotive appeared with *Blue Funnel Line* on the plates for the naming ceremony in April 1945. These were then removed and replaced by *Blue Funnel Certum Pete Finem*, and that name was retained thereafter. In the last months of steam the locomotive gained a reputation for fast running and was recorded at 106mph on 26 June 1967, one month before withdrawal, which suggests that the locomotives still rode well even if they were run down; such performances were much appreciated by the masses of enthusiasts witnessing the end of Southern steam. *J. H. Bird*

Right:
No 21C14 was named *Nederland Line* on 27 November 1945, together with No 21C15 *Rotterdam Lloyd*, at Waterloo by Mr A. F. Bronsig, the shipping company's MD, and this fine action shot shows it at the head of the heavy down 'Devon Belle' between Winchfield and Basingstoke *en route* to Wilton, where it will be exchanged for another member of the class. There is no date for the picture, but it will be after May 1949, when it became No 35014. *Rail Archive Stephenson, C. J. Grose*

Below:
Now with its BR number on the smokebox and still in Malachite Green, *Nederland Line* is seen receiving attention at Eastleigh shed on 16 September 1950. This locomotive was used for haulage comparison trials against 'Lord Nelson' and 'King Arthur' locomotives on the West of England line, where it hauled 16-coach loads. It has its 1949-modified cab, and was originally fitted with short deflectors when new. *Rail Archive Stephenson, W. Rogerson*

21C14 *Nederland Line*	
Renumbered:	35014, May 1949
New:	February 1945
Rebuilt:	July 1956
Mileage, unrebuilt:	516,811
Allocations:	Nine Elms when new; Exmouth Junction, 13 May 1954; Bournemouth, 10 August 1954; Stewarts Lane, 4 June 1955; Nine Elms, 5 June 1956; Weymouth, 14 September 1964
Liveries:	Black when new; Malachite Green, November 1945; BR Brunswick Green, August 1951
Withdrawn:	March 1967
Total mileage:	1,062,394
Fate:	Scrapped by J. Cashmore, Newport, September 1967

Above:
It was unusual to see 'Merchant Navies' double-heading, but here we see *Nederland Line* piloting Class S15 No 30845 away from Seaton Junction on 14 July 1964 at the head of the 2.8pm Axminster to Exeter Central service. *W. L. Underhay*

Right:
No 35014 is ready to leave Nine Elms shed for its next duty on 8 April 1964. The state of the yard indicates that there must have been great difficulties in getting people to work at London steam sheds at that time. *Gavin Morrison*

Right:
In May 1964 No 35014 passes the level crossing at Poole that used to cause so much road chaos before the flyover was built. The picture also shows the very sharp curve out of the station to the east. There was half a mile of level track before the start of Parkstone Bank at around 1 in 60. *E. Thomas*

Left:
The signals are clear for the departure of *Nederland Line* from Bournemouth Central with an up afternoon express for Waterloo on 1 September 1965. The locomotive's external condition was quite normal for Bournemouth locomotives towards the end of steam. *Gavin Morrison*

Left:
A rear view of the same train, showing the rebodied 5,250-gallon tender attached to No 35014. *Gavin Morrison*

Left:
On 7 September 1965 No 35014 blows off as it passes Worgret Junction, where the Swanage branch joins the main line just to the west of Wareham. This is the Weymouth portion of an up Waterloo express, which will combine at Bournemouth Central with coaches from Bournemouth West. *Gavin Morrison*

Renumbered:	35015, June 1949
New:	March 1945
Rebuilt:	June 1958
Mileage, unrebuilt:	549,706
Allocations:	Nine Elms when new; Stewarts Lane, 5 June 1956; Nine Elms, 14 June 1959; stored unserviceable, 6 January 1964
Liveries:	Black when new; Malachite Green, September 1945; BR Blue, February 1951; BR Brunswick Green, June 1953
Withdrawn:	February 1964
Total mileage:	813,950
Fate:	Scrapped by Slag Reduction Co, Rotherham, December 1964

Above:
Rotterdam Lloyd was named at Waterloo in a joint ceremony with No 21C14 on 27 November 1945, and was selected to head the inaugural 'Devon Belle' Pullman in both directions between Waterloo and Wilton on 20 June 1947. At the head of the down 'Bournemouth Belle' in that year, *Rotterdam Lloyd* passes the west end of Wimbledon on its non-stop journey to Southampton. *Rail Archive Stephenson, C. R. L. Coles*

Above:
After servicing, *Belgian Marine* has backed down to Bournemouth West station and is ready to leave. On the left is Ivatt 2-6-2T No 41275 on carriage shunting duties, while on the right is another Ivatt, No 41204, ready to leave with a local train for the former Somerset & Dorset line.
Gavin Morrison

Centre right:
For no logical reason *Belgian Marine* was one of my favourite members of the class, so I have included a few extra pictures. On 12 September 1965 – a year after the picture at Eastleigh featured earlier – the external condition of the engine has deteriorated dramatically, and it has lost its front number plate.
With plenty of steam to spare, the locomotive drifts into Pokesdown, 2 miles east of Bournemouth Central, with an up express for Waterloo.
Gavin Morrison

Right:
This is a rear view of the same train at Pokesdown, still blowing off. There should be no slipping on starting as the gradient drops at 1 in 99 towards Christchurch for just over a mile.
Gavin Morrison

Right:
British India Line was diagrammed to work the first postwar 'Bournemouth Belle' on 7 October 1946, and the immaculate locomotive in its Malachite Green livery is shown at Southampton Central together with the Mayor and other dignitaries. The crew are far too busy filling the tender to listen to any speeches, and it is to be hoped that the civic party moved before the bag was pushed back!
F. Moss

Above:
British India Line was different from the others in that it was originally fitted with fabricated coupled wheels, but in April 1947 these were exchanged for the cast type. It was another locomotive selected for the Locomotive Exchanges of 1948, for the Waterloo-Exeter test runs. Here with its modified cab and Brunswick Green livery, it is about to leave Waterloo on the down 'Atlantic Coast Express' in 1951. In 1952 it was attached to a self-weighing tender for around three months. *Rail Archive Stephenson, C. R. L. Coles*

21C18 *British India Line*

Renumbered:	May 1948
New:	May 1945
Rebuilt:	February 1956
Mileage, unrebuilt:	504,900
Allocations:	Nine Elms when new; Bournemouth, 24 November 1960; Nine Elms, 17 January 1961
Liveries:	Black when new; Malachite Green, August 1945; BR Blue, September 1949; BR Brunswick Green, July 1951
Withdrawn:	August 1964
Total mileage:	956,544
Fate:	Preserved in 1980, but unrestored by 2007

Right:
Two months after rebuilding, with the small BR emblem on the tender and in immaculate condition, *British India Line* heads the down 'Bournemouth Belle' near Hinton Admiral on 2 April 1956. *Rail Archive Stephenson, D. M. C. Hepburne-Scott*

Below:
This superbly atmospheric picture at the east end of Bournemouth Central sees *British India Line* ready to leave with the up 'Bournemouth Belle' (12 Pullmans and a bogie van) on 17 August 1958. As a rebuild there were minor differences between No 35018 and the others, one of which was that the sand fillers were higher, as can be seen. 'King Arthur' 4-6-0 No 30783 *Sir Gillemere* is ready to follow the Pullman with a special fitted freight. *C. P. Boocock*

21C19 *French Line CGT*

Renumbered:	35019, April 1948
New:	June 1945
Mileage, unrebuilt:	617,368
Allocations:	Nine Elms when new; Weymouth, 4 September 1964
Liveries:	Black when new; Malachite Green, September 1945; BR Blue, January 1950; BR Brunswick Green, June 1951
Withdrawn:	5 September 1965
Total mileage:	947,344
Fate:	Scrapped by J. Cashmore, Newport, January 1966

Below:
French Line CGT, photographed at the back of Eastleigh shed, appears to be fresh from Eastleigh Works in the Malachite Green livery, which dates the picture to the end of 1945. This locomotive took part in the Locomotive Exchanges of 1948, was attached to LMS tender No 10219, and had a Flaman speed recorder fitted. It suffered firebox problems after two days working between King's Cross and Leeds, but after repairs it worked between Paddington and Plymouth. It is fitted with small deflectors, but has lost the tall casing in front of the cylinders. *Rail Archive Stephenson, A. W. Croughton*

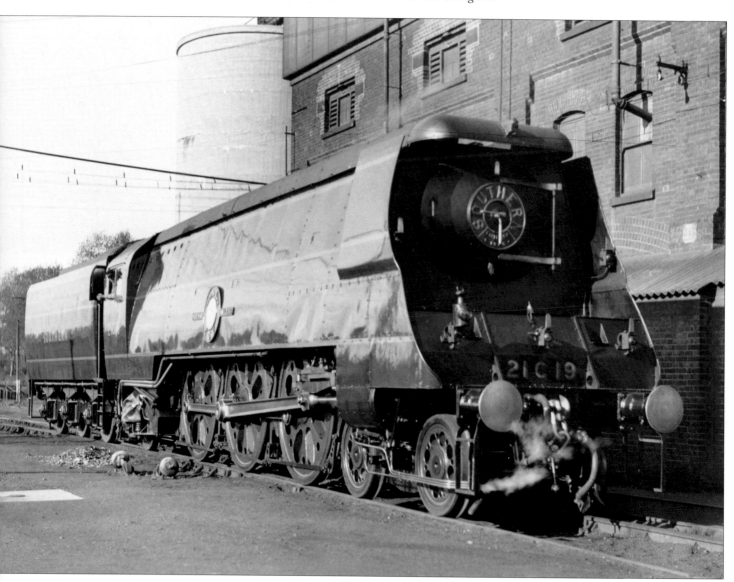

Above right:
Now in BR Brunswick Green livery and with larger deflectors, No 35019 pulls away from Axminster with a down Waterloo-Plymouth Friary express on 26 August 1956. For the last 6 months of 1951 No 35019 ran with a single-nozzle blastpipe and chimney, but the multi-nozzle version was reinstalled in January 1952. *L. Marshall*

Right:
The external condition of *French Line CGT* does credit to Weymouth shed as it passes Deepcut at the head of a down Waterloo-Bournemouth express on 20 May 1965. Four months later it was put into store at Weymouth and withdrawn.
Rail Archive Stephenson, D. M. C. Hepburne-Scott

21C20 *Bibby Line*

Renumbered:	35020, May 1948
New:	June 1945
Mileage, unrebuilt:	507,958
Allocations:	Nine Elms when new; Weymouth, 14 September 1964
Liveries:	Black when new; Malachite Green, August 1945; BR Blue, May 1950; BR Brunswick Green, June 1952
Withdrawn:	February 1965
Total mileage:	981,479
Fate:	Scrapped at Eastleigh Works, March 1965, the only member of the class to be scrapped there

Above:
Bibby Line was unique within the class for carrying the very large smoke deflectors seen here as it storms along near Pirbright Junction at the head of an up express from the West of England. Of particular interest is the fact that it has been renumbered 35020, but still carries the smokebox roundel and the number painted above the buffer beam, while 'Southern' remains on the tender. The exact date is not known, but is probably the second half of 1948.
Rail Archive Stephenson, C. J. Rose

Left:
Bibby Line, seen here at Bournemouth Central in September 1949, had been prepared for the Locomotive Exchanges in 1948, but in fact never took part. The locomotive's main claim to fame was the fracturing of the crank axle when it was travelling between 70 and 80mph approaching Crewkerne on 24 April 1953, causing considerable damage to the station canopy when it was partly derailed. This resulted in the immediate withdrawal of the whole class, and several others were discovered to have defects. This incident helped to hasten the eventual rebuilding of the class.
Ian Allan Library

Left:
A fine panned shot of No 35022 as it speeds past Basingstoke on the 3.20pm Waterloo-Weymouth train on 4 August 1958. *Michael Mensing*

Below:
After its 79-mile non-stop journey from Waterloo, *Holland-America Line*, in immaculate condition, takes water at Southampton Central at the head of the down 'Bournemouth Belle' on 12 September 1964. *Gavin Morrison*

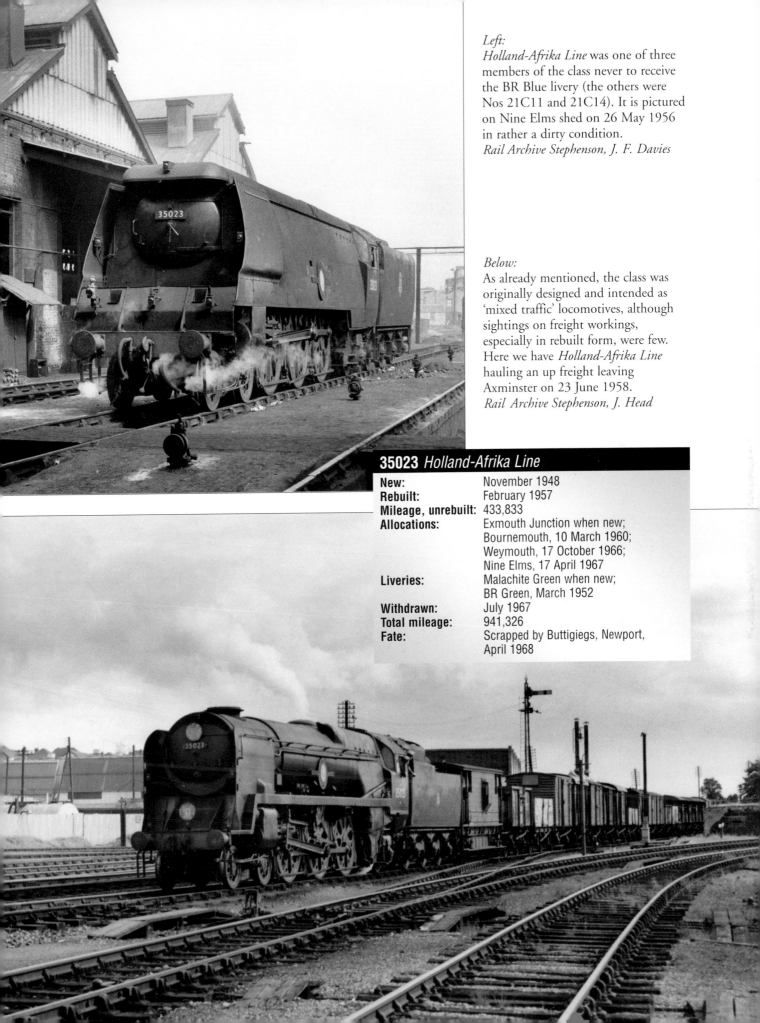

Left:
Holland-Afrika Line was one of three members of the class never to receive the BR Blue livery (the others were Nos 21C11 and 21C14). It is pictured on Nine Elms shed on 26 May 1956 in rather a dirty condition.
Rail Archive Stephenson, J. F. Davies

Below:
As already mentioned, the class was originally designed and intended as 'mixed traffic' locomotives, although sightings on freight workings, especially in rebuilt form, were few. Here we have *Holland-Afrika Line* hauling an up freight leaving Axminster on 23 June 1958.
Rail Archive Stephenson, J. Head

35023 *Holland-Afrika Line*

New:	November 1948
Rebuilt:	February 1957
Mileage, unrebuilt:	433,833
Allocations:	Exmouth Junction when new; Bournemouth, 10 March 1960; Weymouth, 17 October 1966; Nine Elms, 17 April 1967
Liveries:	Malachite Green when new; BR Green, March 1952
Withdrawn:	July 1967
Total mileage:	941,326
Fate:	Scrapped by Buttigiegs, Newport, April 1968

Above:
Holland-Afrika Line coasts through St Denys on the outskirts of Southampton under clear signals with the down 'Bournemouth Belle' on 1 September 1964, at the end of 21 miles of downhill gradients. *M. Dunnett*

Left:
The following week, No 35023 is still on the 'Bournemouth Belle' duty and is seen being prepared for the up working in the sidings at Bournemouth West Junction on 9 September 1964. *Gavin Morrison*

Right:
Holland-Afrika Line lasted to the end of Southern steam on Sunday 9 July 1967. With the depressing message chalked on the smokebox, No 35023 passes through Farnborough for the last time on a down train. *G. P. Cooper*

Left:
This superb action shot shows *Port Line* passing Folkestone Junction at the head of a heavy up Dover Marine-Victoria boat train on 7 June 1954. Still allocated to Stewarts Lane, the locomotive is obviously not receiving the special care it got when regularly employed on the 'Golden Arrow' Pullman, which by this time had become the preserve of 'Britannias' Nos 70004 *William Shakespeare* and 70014 *Iron Duke. Rail Archive Stephenson, T. G. Hepburn*

Below:
In April 1959 the rebuilt *Port Line* was selected for Royal Train duty, when it worked from Windsor to Hamworthy Junction. A couple of years later, on 29 September 1961, it is seen on Eastleigh shed in clean, but not Royal, condition, awaiting a visit to the works for a light intermediate repair. *Gavin Morrison*

Above:
This very fine action shot shows *Clan Line* recovering from a signal check at Lyndhurst Road on the up 13.25 Weymouth-Waterloo train on 2 January 1967. Obviously cleaners were in very short supply at Weymouth at this period! *J. H. Bird*

Right:
In sharp contrast to the previous picture, *Clan Line* is now in fine external condition as it passes St Denys with BR Southern Region's 'Farewell to Steam' special on 2 July 1967. *Brian Stephenson*

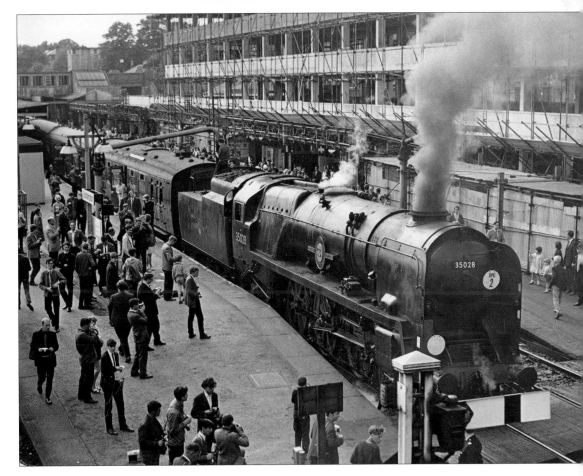

Right:
That July day was a sad one, especially for the enthusiasts who had enjoyed the high-speed performances on the Bournemouth line in the last months by the crews of the Bulleid 'Pacifics'. This picture portrays the occasion well as *Clan Line* takes water at Southampton for the last time in BR ownership. Seven years were to pass before No 35028 reappeared on the BR network on 27 April 1974, since when it has been one of the most regular and consistent performers on the network. *E. Knight*

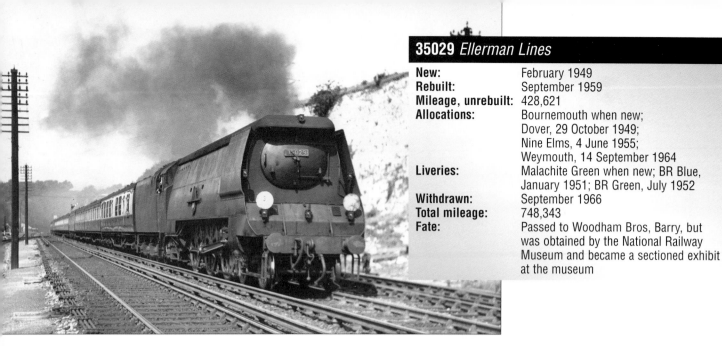

35029 *Ellerman Lines*

New:	February 1949
Rebuilt:	September 1959
Mileage, unrebuilt:	428,621
Allocations:	Bournemouth when new; Dover, 29 October 1949; Nine Elms, 4 June 1955; Weymouth, 14 September 1964
Liveries:	Malachite Green when new; BR Blue, January 1951; BR Green, July 1952
Withdrawn:	September 1966
Total mileage	748,343
Fate:	Passed to Woodham Bros, Barry, but was obtained by the National Railway Museum and became a sectioned exhibit at the museum

Above left:
This powerful action shot shows No 35029 passing Knockholt with a down boat train, prior to being named on 1 March 1951 at Southampton Docks. It appears to be in Malachite Green livery under all the grime. *Rail Archive Stephenson, F. R. Hebron*

Left:
Now in the BR Blue livery, *Ellerman Lines* rounds the curve on the Bickley Loop and joins the main line to Victoria at the head of the Paris-London 'Night Ferry' on 11 August 1951. *Brian Morrison*

The Locomotive Exchanges of 1948

We now live in an age where we can see the same DMUs – Class 158s, for example – or Class 66 locomotives virtually anywhere in the country from Wick to Penzance. By contrast, the Locomotive Exchanges of 1948 must have been very exciting times for the enthusiasts of the day and professional railwaymen alike, as locomotives at that time seldom wandered from their own lines and routes. Much has been written about the trials over the years, but an album on the 'Merchant Navies' would not be complete without a small section on the Exchanges. The Southern Region selected locomotives Nos 35017,

35018 and 35019, with No 35020 as spare. All were fitted with speed recorders and Stanier tenders, as water scoops were needed, except for No 35018, which was trialled on the Southern, so did not change tenders. No 35019 was trialled between Paddington and Plymouth, and between King's Cross and Leeds, No 35017 worked Euston-Carlisle and King's Cross-Leeds, and No 35018 ran between Waterloo and Exeter. The locomotives showed all their good features, rode well, steamed freely, but suffered many small faults, and as always gave high coal and water consumption.

Right:
No 35019 *French Line CGT* must have presented a colourful sight as it left Paddington on the 1.30pm train to Plymouth on the first day of the trials, 19 April 1948 – the locomotive is in Malachite Green, with a Black tender and Chocolate and Cream coaches. *Rail Archive Stephenson, F. R. Hebron*

Below:
On 28 April 1948 No 35019, proudly displaying its 'Southern' roundel on Western Region territory, is watched by a group of railwaymen at Westbourne Park as it approaches Paddington at the head of the 1.44pm train from Plymouth. *Rail Archive Stephenson, F. R. Hebron*

Above:
An inspector (in bowler hat) and other railwaymen gaze at *French Line CGT* as it poses alongside the signal box at the end of the platforms at King's Cross and prepares to leave for Leeds on 17 May 1948. As there is no dynamometer car this was only a pre-test run. There does not appear to be a single enthusiast at the platform end to witness the sight – how times have changed! *Rail Archive Stephenson, A. W. Croughton*

Below:
This appears to be the same train as in the previous picture. No 35019 is now at Peterborough North, where it is the centre of attention. It seems that the photographer must have travelled on the train and escaped the notice of the policeman to get this shot from the platform end. The locomotive failed the next day on the up working. *Rail Archive Stephenson, A. W. Croughton*

Left:
This fine portrait shows No 35005 *Canadian Pacific* in BR Green livery on the turntable at Nine Elms shed on 15 June 1957. It had been fitted with a Berkley mechanical stoker and Flaman speed recorder in April 1948 and carried out trials, eventually going to Rugby testing station in March 1950. The stoker was not found to give any real benefits and was removed. The locomotive suffered a major chain drive failure in September 1950, causing considerable damage to the oil bath and motion. *Rail Archive Stephenson, J. F. Davies*

'Merchant Navies' on shed

Left:
During the last week of steam on the Southern I don't expect the foreman at Nine Elms would have bothered about these two enthusiasts, probably visiting for the last time. *Clan Line* is the locomotive in the background.
Ian Allan Library

Below:
Not looking in the best of external condition, *Royal Mail* is ready to leave Nine Elms for its next duty out of Waterloo on 8 April 1964.
Gavin Morrison

Right:
The special called at Skipton to pick up passengers and take water before heading for Carnforth. *Gavin Morrison*

Below:
Having given the passengers a run that few had ever experienced from Carnforth to Grayrigg summit in 22min 55sec at 60mph, speed increased and we shot over Dillicar troughs at 82.5mph and started the climb to Shap summit at 77.5mph. Speed was still 75mph approaching Scout Green before a plume of smoke was seen near the summit, which brought us to a stand at Shap Wells, where the loco is seen blowing off impatiently after all that hard work. It was a great disappointment to the crew, ruining what could have been one of the fastest runs from Carnforth to the summit. Whether it was bad control or somebody not wanting the LMS Pacific performances being challenged, we will never know. *H. Malham, author's collection*

Right:
At the start of the memorable return trip over the Settle & Carlisle line, *United States Lines* gleams in the evening sunshine as it pulls out of Carlisle. The 20-minute-late departure gave the crew the incentive for the superb performances. *J. Hirst, author's collection*

Left:
Ais Gill summit is in sight for *United States Lines*, which, was travelling at 50mph with its nine-coach load. I was fortunate to be travelling on the footplate, and can vouch for the fact that much of the credit should be given to Fireman Seaby.
H. Malham, author's collection

Centre left:
No 35026 *Lamport & Holt Line*, on the Warwickshire Railway Society's 'Aberdonian' special of 26 June 1966, restarts from an unscheduled signal stop just outside Doncaster, having taken over from 'A3' No 4472 *Flying Scotsman*. The Inspector (with hat) can be seen looking out of the cab. *Gavin Morrison*

Below left:
Lamport & Holt Line appeared on several specials in the north towards the end of 1966. On 22 October, having taken over at York from *Flying Scotsman*, No 35026 heads north along the East Coast Main Line 'racing track' near Beningbrough on its way to Newcastle. *Gavin Morrison*

Above right:
On 20 November 1966 *Lamport & Holt Line* makes a spectacular passage through Chinley East Junction with a 'Williams Deacon's Bank Club' special, while the permanent way gang look on in astonishment. The special is travelling via the Hope Valley on its way to Sheffield and Doncaster, and eventually north to Newcastle.
Gavin Morrison

Right:
The same special crosses the River Don, just to the north of Doncaster, on its way to Newcastle.
Gavin Morrison

Right:
This Stephenson Locomotive Society special on 23 May 1965 originated at Birmingham Snow Hill and travelled via Salisbury to Exeter, returning via Westbury. It started with 'Battle of Britain' No 34051 *Winston Churchill* as far as Salisbury, where No 35017 *Belgian Marine* took over for a lively run to Exeter. It is seen at Exeter receiving attention from the driver before leaving for Westbury, where ex-Great Western 'Castle' No 7029 *Clun Castle* took over and gave a lacklustre performance back to Birmingham. A North British Type 2 diesel is on the left. *Gavin Morrison*

Below:
A Locomotive Club of Great Britain special, 'The East Devon Railtour', headed by No 35022, pauses at Axminster on 28 February 1965. The tour then visited the branches to Lyme Regis, Sidmouth, Budleigh Salterton and Exmouth before heading for Exeter Central. No 35022 then returned to Waterloo on what was advertised as the last 'Merchant Navy' working from Exeter Central. *Gavin Morrison*

Right:
After several postponements and many 'last' specials, the life of one of England's best-loved lines, the Somerset & Dorset Joint, finally ended on Sunday 6 March 1966. On Saturday 5 March the LCGB ran a farewell special, which arrived at Templecombe headed by an immaculate *Clan Line*, seen here pulling the train forward before reversing and heading off to Evercreech Junction behind two Ivatt 2-6-2Ts, Nos 41249 and 41307. Unrebuilt Bulleid 'Pacifics' Nos 34006 *Bude* and No 34057 *Biggin Hill* were waiting in the centre road at Evercreech to take over the train to Bath Green Park. More specials were run on the Sunday, with *Clan Line* again involved, this time hauling a special from Waterloo via Bournemouth to Templecombe.
Gavin Morrison

Right:
It's journey's end for the Southern Counties Touring Society special 'The Southern Wanderer', headed by No 35023 *Holland-Afrika Line*. The train is seen at Platform 2 at Victoria after arriving from Templecombe via the LSWR main line and East Putney on 28 March 1965. *Brian Stephenson*

Left:
A visit by a 'Merchant Navy' to York occurred on 11 October 1964, when No 35007 *Aberdeen Commonwealth* arrived from King's Cross. The tour was originally to have been hauled by a 'Princess Coronation', but they had all been withdrawn during the previous month. Here we see the return working having just passed Chaloners Whin Junction, south of York, on the now closed section of the East Coast Main Line. *Gavin Morrison*

Above:
The southern section of the Somerset & Dorset Joint line was normally out of bounds to 'Merchant Navies', but special dispensation was given for them to be used on specials in the last months. The LCGB's 'Mendip Merchantman Rail Tour', behind No 35011 *General Steam Navigation*, passes Shillingstone station heading for Templecombe on 1 January 1966. *Gavin Morrison*

Left:
General Steam Navigation has just arrived at Broadstone with what was originally intended as a last Somerset & Dorset tour on 2 January 1966. The train had originated at Waterloo, and a locomotive change took place here, with Class 'U' 2-6-0 No 31639 and 'West Country' No 34015 *Exmouth* taking over from the 'Merchant Navy' to Bath. It was a very cold morning and the platform was very slippery, as is being well demonstrated by the gentleman at the bottom of the platform ramp – note the complete lack of concern at his misfortune by all the other enthusiasts intent on getting their pictures! *Gavin Morrison*

Above:
Prior to its preservation and its trips on Network Rail, No 35005 *Canadian Pacific* is seen in immaculate condition on pre-withdrawal rail tour duties heading across Salisbury Plain near Warminster with a Warwickshire Railway Society special bound for Swindon on 23 May 1965.
Brian Stephenson

Right:
No 35030 *Elder Dempster Lines* heads through unfamiliar territory for the class as it climbs towards Chorleywood with the LCGB's 'Great Central Rail Tour' on 3 September 1966.
Brian Stephenson

Ten members of the class – Nos 35005/6/9/10/11/18/22/27/28/29 – have passed into preservation, which out of a class of 30 must surely be considered slightly excessive. Forty years after the end of Southern Region steam, Nos 35005 and 35028 have run specials on the main line, while No 35027 has been active on preserved lines.

Preservation

Above and left:
One inactive member is No 35029 *Ellerman Lines*, which was rescued from Woodham's scrapyard at Barry in 1974, six years after withdrawal, to become a major exhibit at the National Railway Museum, where it was very skilfully sectioned and eventually placed on electrically operated rollers to show visitors how the motion worked, all the other parts being labelled and explained. It arrived by road on a low-loader on 16 September 1975, wrapped in blue sheeting. *Gavin Morrison*

Left:
The following day No 35029 was moved onto the turntable in the main exhibition hall and placed in position; it has since been relocated within the museum. *Both Gavin Morrison*

Right:
In the 1970s *Clan Line* was very active over quite a wide area, but is now mainly operated in the south. This rather unusual view shows it emerging from Windmill Lane Tunnel (104 yards) just to the west of Chester General station, at the head of the 'Red Rose' special from Hereford on 28 April 1979. *Gavin Morrison*

Above:
Clan Line took part in the Stockton &
Darlington 150 celebrations in 1975,
and was also present at the Liverpool &
Manchester celebrations at Bold
Colliery in 1980. It is seen here at
Manchester Victoria, returning from
the festivities on 9 June. In front is
the NRM's 'Schools' class No 925
Cheltenham, with LMS 0-6-0T
No 7298 leading the line-up.
No doubt during its allocation to the
South Eastern Division as an unrebuilt
locomotive it was piloted by a 'Schools',
although it is unlikely to have happened
in rebuilt form on the South Western
Division. *Gavin Morrison*

Left:
A Cravens DMU heading for Shaw
overtakes *Clan Line* as it climbs the 1 in
59/47 of Miles Platting Bank out of
Manchester Victoria on 21 June 1980 –
it was not exactly struggling as it was
receiving assistance at the rear from a
Class 25 Type 2 diesel. *Gavin Morrison*

Above:
Canadian Pacific has also travelled widely over Network Rail since restoration, as well as visiting many preserved lines. During a spell on the East Lancashire Railway it is seen arriving at Ramsbottom with the 11.00 service from Rawtenstall to Bury on 11 August 1991. The 38F shedplate did not exist in BR days. *Canadian Pacific* was painted in lined BR Blue livery during its first years in active preservation, and while this was not authentic it looked very fine, although not as striking as an unrebuilt example would have done.
B. Dobbs

Right:
Canadian Pacific arrives at Bury Bolton Street on the East Lancashire Railway with the 10.00 train from Rawtenstall on 3 August 1991. Repainted in green it has returned to Southern metals on the Mid-Hants Railway
B. Dobbs

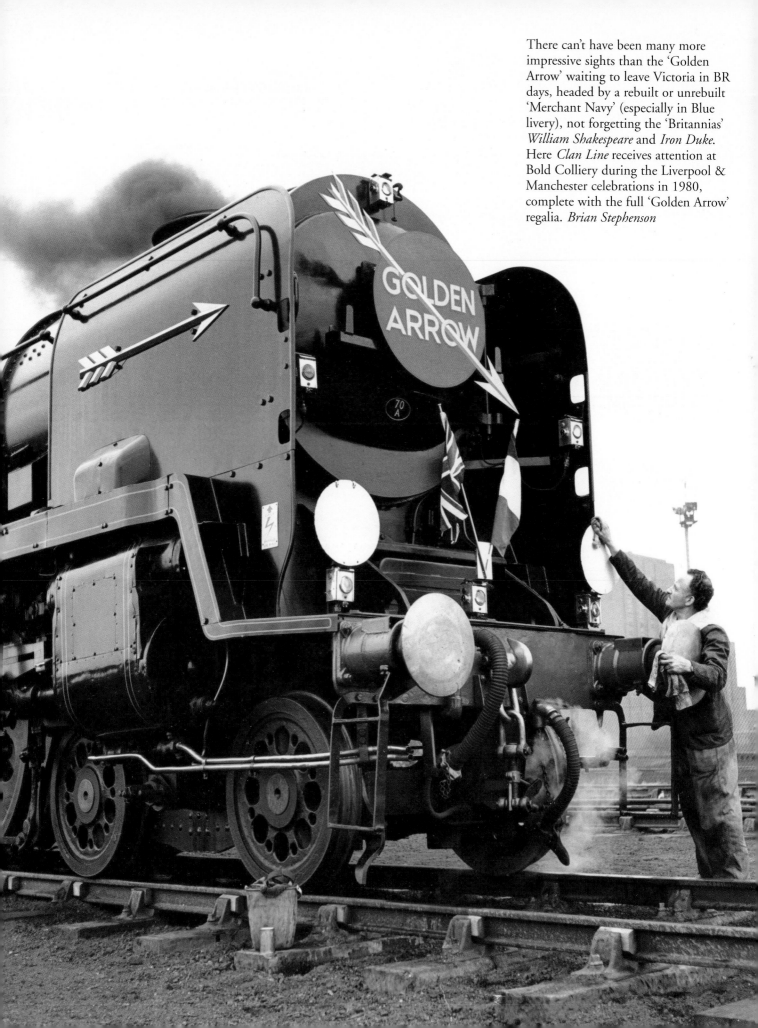

There can't have been many more impressive sights than the 'Golden Arrow' waiting to leave Victoria in BR days, headed by a rebuilt or unrebuilt 'Merchant Navy' (especially in Blue livery), not forgetting the 'Britannias' *William Shakespeare* and *Iron Duke*. Here *Clan Line* receives attention at Bold Colliery during the Liverpool & Manchester celebrations in 1980, complete with the full 'Golden Arrow' regalia. *Brian Stephenson*